D1275942

KENNETH NOLAND
MAJOR WORKS

RICHARD H. LOVE

Haase-Mumm Publishing Company, Inc.

Chicago

EXHIBITION ITINERARY:
R.H. LOVE MODERN,
CHICAGO, IL   May 3-June 21, 1986
THE BUTLER INSTITUTE OF AMERICAN ART,
YOUNGSTOWN, OH   July 20-August 31, 1986
HUNTER MUSEUM OF ART,
CHATTANOOGA, TN November 9, 1986-January 4, 1987
LOCH HAVEN ART CENTER,
ORLANDO, FL   March 15-May 3, 1987
THE ASHEVILLE ART MUSEUM,
ASHEVILLE, NC   May 19-July 5, 1987
MUSKEGON MUSEUM OF ART,
MUSKEGON, MI   August 1-September 13, 1987
SPRINGFIELD ART MUSEUM,
SPRINGFIELD, MO   October 18-December 13, 1987

©1986, R.H. Love. All rights reserved.
No part of this work may be reproduced or transmitted in any
form or by any means, electronic, graphic or mechanical,
including photocopying, taping, and recording or by any
information storage and retrieval system, without written
permission of the publisher. Any such unauthorized use may be
subject to the sanctions under the copyright laws of the United
States.

Published by the Haase-Mumm Publishing Company, Inc.,
Chicago
Distributed by the Amart Book and Catalog Distributing
Company, Inc.
100 East Ohio Street, Room B-20, Chicago, IL 60611
Printed in the United States of America
First Edition.

Library of Congress Cataloging-in-Publication Data

Love, Richard H.
    Kenneth Noland, major works.

    Bibliography: p.
    1. Noland, Kenneth, 1924 - —Exhibitions.
2. Noland, Kenneth, 1924- —Criticism and
interpretation. I. Title.
ND237.N594A4 1986   759.13   86-9983
ISBN 0-940114-21-6

Kenneth Noland,
Master of Modern Color

Surely at one time or another everyone has been captivated by the experience of a colorful sunset, or the translucent hues of flowers in the sunlight, or the flickering surface of a smooth rock in a stream, or the iridescent brilliance of spilled oil on rain-soaked concrete, or the dense opacity of a freshly ploughed field, or the vaporous luminescence of fog rising into the atmosphere, or . . . indeed, how many of these perceptually stimulating combinations of colors which we find in nature are actually commonplace, albeit unique, experiences. The answer is that no one could count them all, and when one is confronted with a new color-bearing form in nature — say a saltwater tropical fish or a glimpse of matter through a high-powered microscope — he is perceptually surprised, even fascinated, but never critical of nature. Indeed, who would think of finding fault with the tonal transitions of a purple orchid or Jack Frost's silvery compositions on a frozen window pane? Man not only accepts the phenomena of color in nature but revels in it, photographs it, poeticizes it, analyzes it, and theorizes it; in short, he objectifies it and subjectifies it — that is, when he finds it in nature.

But how does one react when man manipulates color outside of nature, namely for the sake of art? When manifested within this totally subjective realm, color is distinctly no longer the product of nature but of man and for man's purpose. Accordingly, placed into this milieu, he conjures up significant justification to criticize his product because it always falls short of nature's — but does it? Can man, the artist, put color (only color) into a perceptual format which functions wholly as aesthetic? Over the past two decades various artists have accepted the challenge and failed miserably, others have mitigated their solutions by subtly disguising their latent mimicry of nature, while a few have been successful in the opinion of most serious critics. One of the most continuously successful in this quest is Kenneth Noland, an artist generally described as a color-field painter. That which Noland has achieved with color is unique because the results of his experiments are consistently successful, unlike the attempts of certain followers. And this exhibition, which features his latest and most dynamic excursions into the expression of color on a two-dimensional surface, serves to confirm another round of success.

Although Noland's art has been some of America's most important color abstraction since the late 1950s, it evolved gradually over a number of years. Born in 1924, Kenneth Noland spent his youth in Asheville, North Carolina.[1] In spite of this basically rural environment, he was taught the value of cultural endeavors by a mother who played the piano and a father who executed quasi-impressionistic oil paintings as an avocation. During World War II, Noland served as a glider pilot and cryptographer, but upon release from the U.S. Air Force, he returned to North Carolina where he became an art student at Black Mountain College.[2] Here he was instructed by Ilya Bolotowsky, an abstract painter who was born in Petrograd (present-day Leningrad), Russia, and became a naturalized American citizen in 1929. Having traveled in Europe, Bolo (as Noland referred to him in later life) was influenced by Piet Mondrian and Joan Miró and then became a member of The Ten with Mark Rothko, Adolph Gottlieb, and others by the mid-1930s. Bolotowsky was also a charter member of the American Abstract Artists (1936) and a co-founder of the Federation of Modern Painters and Sculptors.[3]

When Noland began his studies at Black Mountain, Bolotowsky was the acting head of the art department because Joseph Albers, the official head, was temporarily on leave. Born in Westphalia, Germany, Albers studied extensively in Berlin and Essen. Reflecting the influence of Cézanne and Cubism, he had been an art teacher in Germany and also had studied at the Weimar Bauhaus where he later became a member of the faculty. During the 1930s, his experiments in perception (the Step series: depth and surface relationships) were often purposefully unresolved, so he brought them with him to Black Mountain.

Noland spent most of his time at Black Mountain with Bolotowsky. Often in later years he reiterated that his (Bolo's) influence was considerably more significant than Albers's. Noland also made it quite clear that he found Albers's "perceptual insights unbelievable,"[4] but according to Moffett, Bolotowsky stood as "the link between Noland's art and European geometric abstraction — especially De Stijl [a Dutch art movement and magazine begun in 1917 by Theo van Doesburg and Piet Mondrian]."[5] So it was that Bolotowsky laid much of the foundation for Noland's later art, introducing him to shaped canvases and employing contrasting color planes and bands in geometric configurations to arrive at pictorial solutions. Working under Bolotowsky, Noland stressed that Bolotowsky was a liberal master who allowed a good deal of freedom to express oneself within the overall context of geometric abstraction. In summary, Noland learned to think abstractly at Black Mountain via the instruction of both Albers and Bolotowsky, but the latter was the most significant and long-lasting influence. Perhaps the closest Noland came to representational art during these years was Cubism. For the most part he worked directly from a subjective basis. In short, he was trained as a non-objective painter, ignoring all references to the material world save the basic components of art — line, form, color, two-dimensional space, and the harmonic arrangement of these quintessential elements of abstraction. However, it is important to underline the fact that although Noland

Kenneth Noland with his dog Dusty in 1981.

Kenneth Noland outside his studio.

began with non-objective imagery, the influences at Black Mountain College had little to do with the relatively inflexible ideological and metaphysical approaches of first-generation European abstractionists, like Wassily Kandinsky or Kasimir Malevich. To succeed at Black Mountain, Noland's approach was secular, pragmatic, and always disciplined.[6]

Still clinging tenaciously to its reputation as the mecca of modern art, Paris beckoned Noland in 1948. Enrolling at the Academy of La Grande Chaumière, he studied under Ossip Zadkine, an English-trained Russian, who had worked and exhibited successfully in Paris until he fled to New York during Nazi occupation in World War II and then visited Black Mountain College. In Paris, Noland studied the rudiments of sculpture under Zadkine but continued painting in his studio.

Noland and his American friends found mutual support in their quests for modernism in Paris, but most of them were aware that greater advancements in abstraction had been and continued to be made in America than in Europe. Nonetheless, Noland's experience in Europe reaffirmed his admiration for Paul Klee, whose color and expressionist involvement in the execution of his work offered a reasonable alternative to the slick-smooth formal abstraction the former had learned at Black Mountain. Noland searched diligently for more

meaningful expressions via the materials of his imagery, namely the fat and thin pigment, the picture surface, and the relative act of manipulating color. Having offered a certain obligatory student-homage to Picasso and Matisse via a few studies, Noland looked away from Paris and returned to America for fresh inspiration. Before he left, however, his imagery came to reveal the influence of Klee, a fact made quite evident by his first solo exhibition at Galerie R. Creuze in Paris.

Back in America in 1949, Noland became a teacher at the Institute of Contemporary Art in Washington, DC. Continuing work which showed the influence of Klee, Noland returned to Black Mountain in 1950 for the Summer Institute where he met Theodore Stamos, Clement Greenberg, and Helen Frankenthaler; earlier he had made the acquaintance of Elaine and Willem de Kooning, and Buckminster Fuller. Late in 1951 Noland took a teaching job at the Catholic University in Washington, DC.

Leon and Ida Berkowitz founded the Washington Workshop Center of the Arts, a progressive school in Washington, DC, where Noland taught evening classes from 1952 to 1956. It was here that he met Morris Louis, an artist who would figure prominently in his art and career. Sharing many attitudes about art, Noland and Louis spent many hours together, painting, discussing art generally and specifically, and studying the work of others. The art critic Clement Greenberg had introduced Noland to the expressionistic complexities of Jackson Pollock, and by 1952 the influence of "action painting" was evident in Noland's pictures. Within another year, however, larger canvases displayed other tendencies, derived from de Kooning and Franz Kline, stylistic approaches which also appealed to Morris Louis. In 1953 Noland began to use paints manufactured by Leonard Bocour, to whom he had been introduced by Louis.

During a stay in New York in the spring of 1953, Greenberg brought Noland and Louis to the studio of Helen Frankenthaler. This was one of the most important inspirational events of Noland's life (and Louis's), when he became fascinated with a painting by Frankenthaler, known as *Mountains and Sea* (on loan, National Gallery of Art, Washington, DC). Both artists were inspired by Frankenthaler's unprecedented use of wash color (oil pigment thinned with turpentine) on unprimed cotton duck canvas. This wonderfully spontaneous application of soft color resulted in delicate "veils" of hue, another alternative not only to hard-edged geometric abstraction but also to the powerfully personal expression of Pollock.[7] The experience was indelible, although for a short time thereafter Noland and Louis set upon a dual-process, "jam painting, like jazz," in which both men worked on the same picture.

Although they continued a close relationship in Washington and visited New York whenever possible, Noland and Louis each sought different experimental pursuits for about the next three years. During this time Greenberg, from his base in New York, made every effort to encourage both men, to guide them, and to promote their art. For example, in 1954, he organized a show, entitled "Emerging Talent," for Kootz Gallery, in which their art was included. With Greenberg behind them, Noland and Louis had nowhere to go but up. But Noland did not leave Washington, DC, and Greenberg found justification in this self-imposed exile from New York City, the undisputed center of modern art, in that the artist was kept from art community pressures and conformity. In the late 1950s Noland, always gregarious and willing to share information, served as a kind of liaison between the emerging modern art community in Washington, DC, and the established one in New York City, especially that section most influenced by Greenberg.[8] Two solo shows, held respectively in 1957 and the following year at the Tibor de Nagy Gallery in New York, served to establish Noland as a bright talent.

Greenberg's prophecies about Noland came true in the fall of 1959 when a one-man exhibition of his recent work at French and Company in New York revealed a brilliant and unprecedented imagery — concentric circles on open grounds and a couple of other geometric-like motifs.[9] The concentric bands of pure color, executed on unprimed cotton duck canvas, derived from several years of consistent experimentation and discipline, the influences for which came from several European and American sources. Basically, however, it was Noland's ability to balance the formality of a weightless geometric form on an open, seemingly limitless pictorial space with the spontaneous and exuberant handling of the action painters that made his art unique; moreover, this outstanding and unprecedented artistic demonstration placed him immediately in the front rank of contemporary abstract painters.

In one article published only six months after the French and Company show, Greenberg's praise of Noland's work was no less enthusiastic than the lucid description of his innovation. The critic's words bear quotation here because they formed the foundation upon which others would form their opinions: "Noland's motifs do not possess the quality of images; they are present solely in an abstract capacity, as means solely of organizing and galvanizing the picture field . . . . the picture succeeds . . . by re-affirming in the end . . . the limitedness of pictorial space as such, with all its rectangularity and flatness and opacity . . . . The naked fabric acts as a generalizing and unifying field; and at the same time its confessed wovenness and porousness suggest a penetrable, ambiguous plane . . . . Noland's art owes much of its truly phenomenal originality to the way in which it transcends the alternative between the painterly and the geometrical. Perhaps Louis (and Frankenthaler) have set the precedent here, but Noland has confronted the issue more squarely . . . . The benefit that both artists [Louis and Noland] have obtained in exchange is a freshness and immediacy of surface that are without like in contemporary art."[10]

In spite of their complex derivations, Noland's concentric band pictures provided a pictorial format which allowed color to function solely as color, indeed, as a wholly abstract element of art. Like some later motifs, the circles and targets were quite effective in breaking the perceptual relationship of color and form because, as Noland stated, such a form functioned "as a self-canceling structure." He explained: "With structural considerations eliminated I could concentrate on color."[11] Although certain color bands contained more spontaneous pigment manipulation than others, the hue was generally flat — and became flatter — calling attention to the two-dimensional surface in which references to no other element but pure geometric forms are discernible. No pictorial illusion of depth by virtue of overlapping planes (Cubistic or otherwise) created confusion in such a pictorial framework since the simplistic existence of color makes absolutely no secondary implication of nature and serves wholly as an aesthetic expression. The carefully planned juxtaposition of various band widths and their relative hue-bearing qualities provide additional liveliness, tension, vibrancy, and general visual dynamism.

The color-staining procedures employed by Noland and Louis during the years after their encounter with Frankenthaler's oil-wash veil picture,

ICE SHINE 1986
acrylic on canvas 96^{13}/$_{16}$ x 80^{7}/$_{8}$ inches

resulted in consistently flat but bright color areas. Although Noland first experimented with water-soluble dry acrylic pigments, eventually he preferred the commercially prepared oil-based *Magna,* which can be thinned without affecting color intensity and has no diverse affect on unprimed cotton duck canvas.[12] Later, in executing the larger chevron pictures, Noland employed the water-based Ac-quatec color on raw canvas.

In assessing the special qualities which derive from the evolution of Noland's technique, it is important to understand that it emerged during the last years of Abstract Expressionism or "painterly" abstraction, as Greenberg called it.[13] Keeping this in mind, we can see better how Noland's innovative color abstractions evolved more from the influences of classic Pollock than de Kooning or others: the direct *hands-on* approach in the execution of the work is a major factor in Noland's art. The physical response to the canvas surface and direct studio-oriented artistic connection with various materials served the artist as a compelling human expression beyond the tradition of brush, paint, and canvas; a greater personal involvement via the art materials helped to maintain individuality while expanding the potential of the color-bearing motifs. Accordingly, the whole picture surface was more uniformly suc-cessful. Also, this very direct technique tended to mitigate expression-inhibiting formality of geometric motif. As Pollock worked outward in swirls and circles from the center of his image to cover the whole surface of his rectangular canvas, Noland also believed that "the only thing to do would be to focus from the center out."[14] Having learned quite a few lessons from the older master of American abstraction, Noland pursued his imagery in a physical manner, rendering purely abstract forms in a spatially limitless pictorial environment.

By 1960 Noland's motifs consisted primarily of pristine bands of bright color separated by spatial widths of white canvas. What was left of the virtuoso manner or painterly style had been completely abandoned for the staining-soaking method. Taking care to maintain the centrality of the motif on an open field, Noland experimented variously with the outer spandrel areas, switching neutral planes with color and reversing bands. In 1961 Noland moved to New York City. Further experiments resulted in the Cat's Eye pictures consisting of an oval super-imposed on a circle.

Toward the end of 1962, the artist began his famous chevron series. In discussing these, Moffett reports that "Noland does not think in terms of forms or shapes . . . . As regard layout, he is concerned to

Kenneth Noland at the offices of Ediciones Poligrafa, S.A. in Barcelona, Spain, 1985.

SONGS: "LIMEHOUSE BLUES" 1984
acrylic on canvas 86½ x 65¾ inches

relate color to support."[15] The very earliest examples, which continued on somewhat of an experimental basis through 1963, finally reached a relatively distinguishable format by the following year. Also in 1963 Noland moved to South Shaftesbury, Vermont, where he purchased Robert Frost's farm.

As Noland continued his work for the following two decades into the 1980s, he experimented with diamond-shaped pictures, horizontal-stripe pictures, plaid designs, and other formal color-bearing configurations on open spaces. Yet in all of these the chevron seems to remain the most compelling motif, one whose full potential Noland still has not exploited sufficiently. To a less idealistically motivated artist, the target motifs could have carried secondary symbolic references to numerous forms in nature — solar symbols for example; in the same way, one might search for and find aesthetic justification in relating chevrons to various objects and forms in nature; however, it should be emphasized that Noland has never been motivated by traditional symbolism. On the contrary, whether circle, diamond, chevron, or any geometric motif, Noland selected those which offers the least resemblance to nature, so their employment as color-bearing designs on an open ground emancipates color from its ties to matter and propels it into its own aesthetic dimension. In the same way that he demanded centrality from the concentric bands, he placed the early chevrons into a boundless pictorial domain. The well-known picture *Cadmium Radiance* (1963) is an outstanding example.

Further development of the chevron design resulted in the eccentric or asymmetrical chevron pictures in which the motif was tipped to one side and placed off center. Centrality was sacrificed for greater neutral area, albeit the kind which seems to yield less containment of the motif (it falls effortlessly from the picture boundaries) and less symmetrical balance of form within an exclusively perceptual format. In these dynamic works the asymmetrical form which floats untethered outside the boundaries results in an uncharacteristic, though dramatic precariousness. Though frequently successful compositions, these asymmetrical chevrons present a kind of mode ambiguity in that the viewer is hard-pressed psychologically to disassociate its function as an abstract motif from its traditional form and position, a *triangle* tipped on its point — suddenly the most stable canon form in the history of art has been turned upside down on its fulcrum. But in so doing, Noland also eliminated one more inadvertent psychological reference to the material world in his attempt to release color from its material entanglements. Most of these chevron motifs were executed on traditional easel-picture canvas surfaces, the formats of which were aligned to the rectangle or square. Intermediate steps in the evolution of Noland's chevrons resulted in the square, diamond (a square turned on its points), and the elongated diamond, actually a shaped-canvas. By virtue of these different outer boundaries, Noland hoped to stimulate a variety in a viable intercourse

between the color-bearing motif and the neutral field upon which it was executed.

Expansion of the chevron configuration offered countless opportunities. One of the most interesting was the elongated or horizontally oriented chevron. A striking example is the very large *Tropical Zone* (83 x 212½ inches), in which the points of two chevrons are opposed and the diagonal bands stretch uniformly as if pushed together by hidden forces in an effort to level out their otherwise precarious balance. Motivated only by factors of abstraction, Noland's purpose here had little to do with the laws of physics, save the flat surface upon which he painted. Nonetheless, the logical artistic progression in the evolution of the chevron was to straighten the arms of the motif until they became flatter and flatter and eventually straight parallel bands of color that were suspended across a horizontal format. These so-called stripe pictures emerged in 1965, and Noland worked with variations of the motif for several years. According to Moffett, over 200 horizontal band pictures were executed in the late 1960s.[16]

In her outstanding essay published in *Artforum* in 1967, Jane Harrison Cone reminded her readers that Noland's pictures "are about the presenting of an untrammelled experience of color." She went on to explain that his canvases possessed "something new, a quality that I can so far only describe as 'forcing a certain way of seeing color.' "[17] Indeed, his work did force us to see color differently and it helped to generate a whole school of followers, the color-field painters. By this time Noland had become the leading color-field painter, with his work generally accepted as the most innovative and trend-setting and prompting occasional retrospective overviews of his development.[18]

But Noland was reluctant to abandon the chevron form. In the diamond shaped- canvases of the mid-1960s, for example, we find chevrons floating with the points downward or pointing right or left; in any instance, the whole picture surface is covered with color, save a narrow white border edge — in some instances even the border is eliminated on the diamond-shaped structures. In spite of its temporary purge from his oeuvre, it resurfaced (no pun intended).

Perhaps one of the most striking features of the chevron pictures is the fact that the upper ends of the "V's" of color moved directionally (color relationships and often value contrasts heightening the sense of movement) off the top edges of the canvas. In a typical vertical format, the tip of the chevron points toward the floor. In this now quite typical symmetrical placement, the chevrons imply a much larger dimension, the largest part of which carries outside the picture plane. Here the viewer is treated to a special place in the realm of aesthetics, the only spot in the perceptual world where one can experience a glimpse of the convergent point of several magnificent parallel bands of sheer color opulence (like the prismatic tip of an upside down iceberg glistening in the sun), which move in opposing directions toward infinity and beyond our perception and

EARTH MARK 1983
acrylic on canvas 87 x 120¼ inches

comprehension. As the arms move outward from the pictorial registry into a mental aesthetic realm, we are confronted with a new sense of color drama, made perceptually tangible, nonetheless, through a brief encounter with small planes presented by Noland. Like no other painter, Noland offers his viewer a slice of aesthetics which begs contemplation of nth degree sources of color-field relationships, and he thus forces, as Cone stated, "a certain way of seeing color."

Still, we must wonder: if the existence of the chevron motif serves only to manifest color, how must we see its attendant color properties? These diagonal "color belts," to use Michael Fried's early description of the chevrons, have frequently existed as flat color areas.[19] In fact, once Noland reached the Post-Painterly period in his oeuvre, most color bands, whether broken symmetrically into chevrons or stretched out flat, contained little if any tonal modulation or evident brushwork. Part of this owed to Noland's staining technique, but the overall result was bright pigment rendered into fixed tonal densities. Occasionally the staining procedure provided a certain variance in color translucency, but seldom if ever to the extent of the expressively painted bands which made up the early target pictures. Furthermore, raw canvas was eliminated between the chevron arms, thus creating less of a floating sensation between the arms and a greater unit cohesiveness. Indeed, it was Fried who once noted that Noland chose to "relinquish . . . the extremely powerful optical effects he could achieve through floating. . . [various] motifs in bright colors on raw canvas." Fried went on to say that the chevrons "seem to want to emphasize their own flatness, to call attention to the fact they exist on, or are stained into, a flat surface."[20]

But Noland continued his experiments with the chevron over the years, and its hue relationships evolved consistently until now, in the mid-1980s, the bands of the chevrons are no longer constrained by flatness, and the triangle configuration adheres predictably to his traditional vertical-rectangular canvas format. The change is obvious: presently Noland's chevron belts are still sensitive juxtapositions of harmonious hue, but now their elongated parameters vibrate with restlessly sensuous pigment, a yielding vehicle for expression. The difference between these works and the earlier chevron motifs is astounding: even the briefest analysis of Noland's oeuvre proves that he never abandonded the hands-on process of artistic materials, but in these works we find a new dynamism achieved through an unprecedented manipulation of fat and thin pigment. Laying full-bodied but fluid impasto passages over resilient color planes, Noland has created a definite color vibrancy and a scintillating surface quality in some of these color bands, which smack slightly of certain nineteenth-century impressionist techniques and bring to mind "Abstract Impressionism," a term used by some in the mid-1950s.[21] Here however, we find personal expression held in check, relegated as it were to the limits of the medium and contained within the motif.

There is action and energy indeed, but it remains tied to the original quest, to wrench every property from color. It is almost as if Noland has renewed his interest in Pollock and resurrected a new painterly style especially for the chevron motif and its continued thrust in his art.

In some instances the point of the triangle reaches the lower edge of the picture, but in other instances the spandrel areas connect to create a sense of openness in a painted field. In one instance, *Ice Shine* (p. 7), the chevron is a triangle-shaped canvas, a chevron with no field. In most cases, however, these powerful and highly individual chevron bands are harmoniously juxtaposed within their larger pictorial boundaries, leaving ample opportunity for the implication of their continued existence beyond the picture plane. This new major series of chevrons demonstrates outstanding pictorial uniformity, something which is frequently difficult to achieve in the process of abstraction; aside from the varying distances of their projection into the lower part of their rectangular spaces, the chevrons are still symmetrically placed, the bands of color emanating from the right and left upper corners and running downward at a diagonal to a point of convergence.

But color is the compelling factors in these works, so we must return to the true function of the chevrons, the presentment of color. As a painter, Noland need justify fewer and less complex demands of color than nature since the latter has amply proven color's *raison d'être*. Therefore, as man's representative, Noland establishes his proof through art, requiring but one vehicle, one surface type, one medium, even one motif. In some of these new pictures, the effect is reminiscent of certain color properties found in nature. For example, *Songs: "Limehouse Blues"* (p. 9) displays a kind of marblized quality. Upon closer scrutiny, however, we see that Noland's application bears only superficial resemblance to marble; moreover, there is no intended or implied illusion of nature, thus, no equivalence. In fact, not only does his unique color application not imitate nature, but for art's sake rivals it. Perhaps for the sake of rationalization, one could equate the title *Ice Shine* (p. 7) with the picture's striking surface. Yet, we know that Noland's purpose rules out such titular associations with nature. In fact, the sheer color effects and surface qualities of shining ice are purposefully mitigated, rejected as it were, by the strict formality of this work, a chevron-shaped canvas. Another point to be made in this regard is Noland's repetitious use of song titles, once again, an obvious attempt to disassociate the surface effect of the canvas from any found in nature. It should also be pointed out that Noland's use of song titles implies no attempt at synaesthetics, but he believes that music "probably has a great deal to do with some of the expressive quality that's in painting abstractly."[22]

Regardless of the unusual color effects, Noland makes no effort there to conclude or extend the empiricism of Ogden N. Rood or Michel Eugène Chevreul.[23] Noland's always has been and shall probably

SONGS: "SUNRISE SERENADE" 1984
acrylic on canvas 86½ x 61½ inches

always be an intuitive response to color. He has stated that he tries "very much not to determine what [he] might paint on any day, whether light or dark or warm or cool." He adds: "I want the picture to come out of the experience, come out emotionally edited."[24] Owing to the fact that man protracts color beyond the analytical and so-called objective realm of illusion into the subjective realm of abstraction, the more unique an artist can make the properties of color in his rivalry with nature, the more successful his art shall be, so long as abstraction is his motivation. Therefore, because Noland has not altered his employment of the chevron and has added new expression in his medium, these pictures (executed over a period of 2-3 years) display the most successful product of pure color the artist has produced thus far.

When Barbara Rose gave an overview of his work in 1964, she reminded her readers that the "centralized [concentric bands] image was cleansed of the casualness and easy spontaneity of chance floods and brushed flourishes."[25] She concluded: "Noland's paintings, lacking any conceivable association with forms found in nature, are more strictly 'abstract' than either Frankenthaler's — which often suggest landscapes — or Louis's — in which veils and mists of colour may evoke poetic, albeit unspecific, correspondences."[26] Since that time the evolution of Noland's predetermined motifs has precluded the highly individualized spontaneity one might associate with Hofmann and other abstract expressionists, and it has also resulted in continued high levels of abstraction because Noland's pictures remain consistently resistant to interpretation with regard to nature. Once again, to borrow Rose's phrase, Noland "learns from his own experience."[27] And so, although Noland's original chevrons were striking departures from other motifs, the potential of their function as color-bearing forms was greater because in their geometric rigidity and compelling symmetry they imply fewer references to shapes and forms found in nature.

Now, in his new paintings of the mid-1980s, Noland has discovered the chevron's greatest potential: more than ever this non-organic form is mitigated by the primary function of color. No more than boundaries of color within boundaries of color, these V's have surfaces and relative color properties unlike any chevrons from an earlier date. Magnetized by the unprecedented variety of these color surfaces, we are reminded of Greenberg's premise that Noland's "colour counts by its clarity and energy; it is not there neutrally, to be carried by the design and the drawing; it does the carrying itself."[28] Frequently, rich luxurious spatial planes provide an hospitable environment in which these chevrons display their opulescent hues. There are delicate balances of high-key color as in Songs: "What a Difference a Day Makes" (p. 17), but we also find active fluid surfaces like the one in Songs: "Crazy Rhythm" (p. 19). Occasionally chevrons seem to battle for optical recognition, with each plane vibrating to the limits of its boundary, causing the unit form to reverberate in its rectangular space. In other in-

stances the frenzied agitation of the chevron appears quite compatible with its equally energetic surrounding surface.

More than other artists, Noland shows in these works that color has no specific form which man and nature give it, only optical properties: lower-key underlying planes provide a forum upon which color ensembles are found brimming with diffusion, translucency, scintillating energy, opacity, luminescence, vibration, and sheer opulence. Viewed in a raking light, these surfaces are amazingly tactile. Far different from the earliest image which "was cleansed of the casualness and easy spontaneity of chance floods and brushed flourishes," these superb statements project a distinct purpose, variety, and the sumptuousness of color, with its latent optical properties brought to life when exploited by a master. Placed carefully over translucent terraces of hue, pulsating, reverberating lines and crisp plates of color seem to emanate from hidden electronic sources. In a fascinating contrast to Noland's early works, the chevrons of such a painting contain arbitrary jewellike facets which fairly sparkle from the seeming play of an internal light source. In other paintings, like Songs: "Sunrise Serenade" (p. 13), each chevron band competes with its neighbor, struggling to maintain its property uniqueness, but viewed as a unit, the chevron serves as a unifying tonal element within an equally contrasting field. In some instances Noland's new brand of optical dynamism is achieved with fluid swirls and squeegeelike passages of flat, albeit fluid pigment, while in other instances there is a typical hand-on working of the medium as if to discover a new tactile quality in the acrylic color vehicle. In conversations with him, the artist has expressed unbridled enthusiasm for this new manifestation of color: "I worked with medium extenders, gels which weren't milky, so color could be clear and pearlescent. . . . I worked with a squeegee to get certain effects."[29]

In the large diamond picture Periplum (p. 30), 1985, brilliant bands of highly charged pigment pulsate within their boundaries, each an outstanding color statement unto itself. Here three intermediate reddish bands and one apex tend to serve as buffer zones for the three bolder statements in contrasting hues and pigment surfaces. This compelling design stands as a bold and expressive pictorial contrast to the chevrons, but it, too, displays the color continuity Noland seeks in these works. All in all, he has given new purpose and new optical life to his two-dimensional bands of color, most of which are organized into typical Noland-type chevron configurations. Even in one of the earliest examples, Earth Mark, 1983, in which the chevron arms are broadened and the bands fail to project out of the upper register of the picture, there is an obvious indication of things to come, a controlled dynamism as it were, an internal life source of color pigment which fairly bursts from its pictorial confines. And in every instance, these works are far different from the "post-painterly" images which were "cleansed" of their spontaneity and flourishes.

So what do we have in these pictures? Is this

CHIME 1983
acrylic on canvas 85 x 69½ inches

Kenneth Noland with wife Peggy Schiffer and son Sam in
Santa Barbara, California.

SONGS: "WHAT A DIFFERENCE A DAY MAKES" 1984
acrylic on canvas 80¾ x 60 inches

Noland virtuoso? Are these painterly expressions disguised in a vehicular form of geometric abstraction? Has Noland reverted to the painterly abstract dynamics of the early 1950s — in effect, does one find these works reflective of the Neo-Expressionism we have discovered in this period called Post-Modernism? The answer is absolutely, categorically *NO* to all questions. Greenberg, other critics, and Noland himself have been quick to point out the influence of Pollock, whose hands-on art process and personal response to materials was an inspirational starting point. But that is the beginning and end of Noland's abstract expression, for these are not examples of "all-over" action painting; they are outstanding images whose motif still functions as a color-bearing form, only this time with more variety of color and attendant surface than ever before. In these works Noland proves one of his oldest

premises, namely that "handling of materials in an expressive sense, not a gesture sense, was a factor that was a little harder or a little different to get onto — being able to handle it [the medium] loosely and stay in touch with the handling, rather than projecting some symbolic reference into it that was more intellectual."[30] Unlike de Kooning, who clung to figure forms, and unlike Hofmann, who saw the push-pull tension of his work as something symbolic of the inherent force-antiforce qualities of nature, and unlike so many others who manipulate pigment simply for the resultant dynamics of personal expression, Noland, via the continued use of the chevron form, has relegated his unique expression of color to a distinctly non-organic confine, forcing viewers once again to see the scope of color anew, to see color itself, for aesthetic purposes only, for you and me.

Notes

1. Biographical data for this essay is taken from personal interviews with Kenneth Noland and from Kenworth Moffett, *Kenneth Noland* (New York: Harry N. Abrams, Inc., 1977).

2. Martin Duberman, *Black Mountain, An Exploration in Community* (New York: E.P. Dutton & Co., 1972).

3. Naylor, Colin, and Genesis P. Orridge, eds., *Contemporary Artists* (New York: St. Martin's Press, 1977), p. 111.

4. Duberman, p. 70.

5. Moffett, p. 15.

6. Kenneth Noland, interview with Richard H. Love, 29 October 1985. Videorecording, American Art Forum with Richard Love, Chicago.

7. See *Helen Frankenthaler, Paintings on Paper,* exhibition catalog (San Francisco, CA: John Berggruen Gallery, 1986).

8. For a discussion of their early work by Greenberg, see Clement Greenberg, "Louis and Noland," *Art International,* 4, no. 5 (May 1960), pp. 26-29.

9. It should be pointed out here that the motifs shown by Noland at French's also included certain spontaneously executed crosses (crucifix or asterisklike forms) and lozenge shapes, but it was the "compass-drawn concentric bands of flat color" which impressed Greenberg and others.

10. Greenberg, "Louis and Noland," pp. 28-29.

11. Al McConaghan, "Noland Wants His Painting to Exist as Sensation," *Minneapolis Tribune,* 13 March 1966, p. 4.

12. See Moffett, p. 101, note 3, for a discussion of Noland's materials.

13. Clement Greenberg, "After Abstract Expressionism," *Art International,* 6, no. 8 (October 1962), p. 24.

14. "Hitting the Bullseye," *Newsweek,* LIX, no. 16 (16 April 1962), p. 108.

15. Moffett, p. 58.

16. Moffett, p. 72.

17. Jane Harrison Cone, "Kenneth Noland's New Paintings," *Artforum,* 6, no. 3 (November 1967), pp. 36-41.

18. For an interesting overview of Noland's work in the mid-1960s, see Barbara Rose, "Kenneth Noland," *Art International,* 8, nos. 5-6 (Summer 1964).

19. Michael Fried, "New York Letter," *Art International,* 6, no. 8 (October 1962), p. 70.

20. Ibid.

21. This term was used occasionally in reference to Philip Guston's new work (c. 1955), which incorporated a brighter high-key palette and was reminiscent of some of Monet's *Water Lilies,* which had recently been acquired by the Museum of Modern Art. See Dore Ashton, *American Art Since 1945* (New York: Oxford University Press, 1982), p. 48.

22. Kenneth Noland in Paul Cummings, *Artists in Their Own Words* (New York: St. Martin's Press, 1979), p. 149.

23. See Ogden N. Rood, *Modern Chromatics* (New York: D. Appleton and Co., 1881) and M.E. Chevreul, *The Principles of Harmony and Contrast of Colors* (London: Longman, Brown, Green, and Longman, 1855).

24. Noland in *Artists in Their Own Words,* p. 152.

25. Barbara Rose, "Kenneth Noland," p. 58.

26. Ibid.

27. Ibid., p. 60.

28. Greenberg, "Louis and Noland," p. 29.

29. Kenneth Noland, interview with Richard H. Love, April 1986, R.H. Love Galleries Archives, Chicago.

30. Noland in *Artists in Their Own Words,* p. 153.

SONGS: "CRAZY RHYTHM" 1984
acrylic on canvas 97½ x 70 inches

SONGS: "A NIGHT IN TUNISIA" 1984
acrylic on canvas 84 x 60½ inches

TIMES LIGHT 1983
acrylic on canvas 85 x 62 inches

WING 1983
acrylic on canvas 85 x 69 inches

GLOSS 1985
acrylic on canvas 83¾ x 66 inches

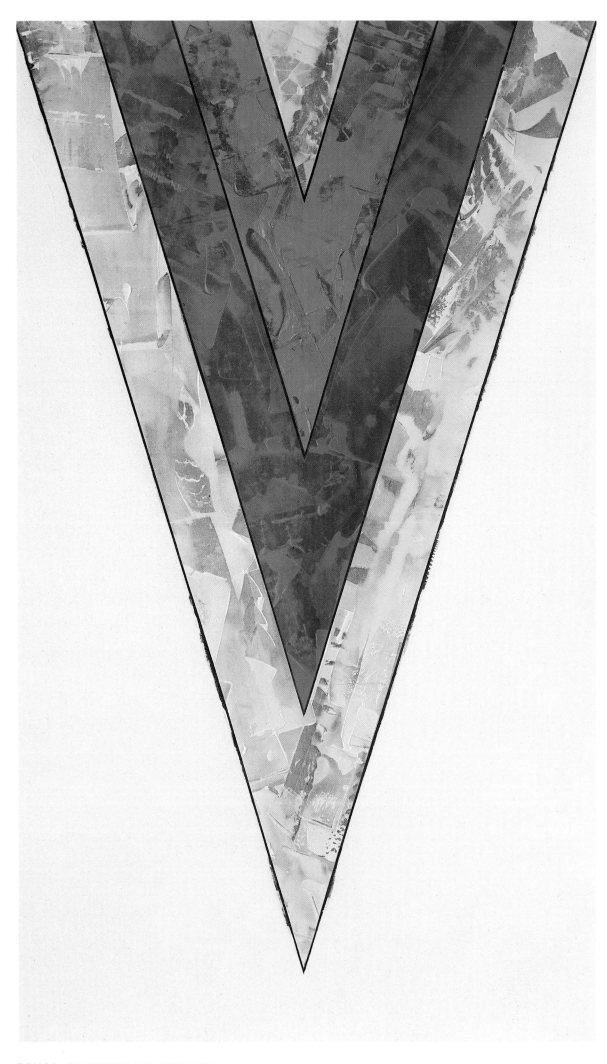

SONGS: "TAKE THE A TRAIN" 1985
acrylic on canvas 119½ x 70½ inches

SONGS: "CHEROKEE" 1984
acrylic on canvas 93½ x 66 inches

SONGS: "NIGHT SONG (JUAN TIZOL)" 1984
acrylic on canvas 86¾ x 61½ inches

SONGS: "SWEET SUE" 1984
acrylic on canvas 86 x 62 inches

SONGS: "UNKNOWN TITLE" 1984
acrylic on canvas 91 x 82¾ inches

SONGS: "SOPHISTICATED LADY" 1984
acrylic on canvas 83¾ x 62 inches

SONGS: "CHICAGO" 1985
acrylic on canvas 51¾ x 81½ inches

PERIPLUM 1985
acrylic on canvas 87 x 214½ inches

INSCRIBE 1984
acrylic on canvas 91 x 82¾ inches

SONGS: "INDIAN LOVE CALL" 1984
acrylic on canvas 87⅞ x 61⅞ inches

EARTH COLORS 1985-86
acrylic on canvas 83⅛ x 71 inches

Major Museum Collections

Albright-Knox Art Gallery, Buffalo, New York.
Art Institute of Chicago, Chicago, Illinois.
Australian National Gallery, Canberra, Australia.
Baltimore Museum of Art, Baltimore, Maryland.
City Art Museum, St. Louis, Missouri.
Columbus Gallery of Fine Arts, Columbus, Ohio.
Corcoran Gallery of Art, Washington, DC.
Des Moines Art Center, Des Moines, Iowa.
Detroit Institute of Fine Arts, Detroit, Michigan.
Fogg Art Museum, Cambridge, Massachusetts.
Gallery of South Australia, Adelaide, Australia.
Solomon R. Guggenheim Museum, New York.
Hara Museum of Contemporary Art, Tokyo, Japan.
Hirshhorn Museum and Sculpture Garden, Washington, DC.
Honolulu Academy of Arts, Honolulu, Hawaii.
Hunter Museum of Art, Chattanooga, Tennessee.
Kunsthaus, Zurich, Switzerland.
Kunstmuseum, Basel, Switzerland.
Kunstsammlung Nordrhein-Westfalen, Düsseldorf, West Germany.
Louisiana Museum, Humlebaek, Denmark.
Milwaukee Art Center, Milwaukee, Wisconsin.
Musée National d'Art Moderne, Central National d'Art et de Culture Georges-Pompidou, Paris, France.
Museum of Fine Arts, Boston, Massachusetts.
Museum of Modern Art, New York.
National Gallery of Art, Washington, DC.
Pasadena Art Museum, Pasadena, California.
Phillips Collection, Washington, DC.
Rose Art Museum, Brandeis University, Waltham, Massachusetts.
Stedelijk Museum, Amsterdam, Holland.
Tate Gallery, London, England.
Walker Art Center, Minneapolis, Minnesota.
Whitney Museum of American Art, New York.

Selected One-Man Exhibitions

Aldrich Museum, Ridgefield, Connecticut, 1980.
André Emmerich Gallery, New York, 1961, 1962, 1963, 1964, 1966, 1967, 1971, 1973, 1975, 1977, 1978, 1980, 1981, 1982, 1983, 1984, 1985, 1986.
David Mirvish Gallery, Toronto, Canada, 1965, 1968, 1974, 1976.
Disputacio de Valencia, Valencia, Spain, 1985.
Douglas Drake Gallery, Kansas City, Missouri, 1982.
Downstairs Gallery, Edmonton, Alberta, Canada, 1982.
French & Co., New York, 1959.
Galerie Alfred Schmela, Düsseldorf, West Germany, 1962, 1964.
Galerie André Emmerich, Zurich, Switzerland, 1973, 1976, 1979, 1982.
Galerie Charles Lienhard, Zurich, Switzerland, 1962.
Galerie Creuze, Paris, France, 1949.
Galerie Daniel Templon, Paris, France, 1976.
Galerie de France, Paris, France, 1984.
Galerie Joan Prats, Barcelona, Spain, 1983, 1984, 1985; New York 1984.
Galerie Lawrence, Paris, France, 1963.
Galerie Neufville, Paris, France, 1961.
Galerie Renée Ziegler, Zurich, Switzerland, 1969.
Galerie Wentzel, Hamburg, West Germany, 1976, 1980; Cologne, West Germany, 1982, 1984.
Galleria Dell'Ariete, Milan, Italy, 1960.
Hokin Gallery, Inc., Bay Harbor Island, Florida, 1983.
Janie C. Lee Gallery, Houston, Texas, 1974.
Jefferson Place Gallery, Washington, DC, 1958, 1960.
The Jewish Museum, New York, 1965.
Kasmin Ltd., London, England, 1963, 1965, 1968, 1970.
"Kenneth Noland: A Retrospective," Solomon R. Guggenheim Museum, New York, 1977; Hirshhorn Museum and Sculpture Garden, and the Corcoran Gallery of Art, Washington, DC, 1977; Toledo Museum of Art, Toledo, Ohio, 1978; Denver Art Museum, Denver, Colorado, 1978.
Lawrence Rubin Gallery, New York, 1969.
Leo Castelli Gallery, New York, 1976, 1980.
Makler Gallery, Philadelphia, Pennsylvania, 1984.
Medici-Berenson Gallery, Bay Harbor Island, Florida, 1978.
Meredith Long & Co., Houston, Texas, 1978.
Museo de Bellas Artes, Bilbao, Spain, 1985.
The New Gallery, Bennington College, Bennington, Vermont, 1961.
Nicholas Wilder Galery, Los Angeles, California, 1966.
Rutland Gallery, London, England, 1974.
School of Visual Arts Gallery, New York, 1975, 1982.
Thomas Segal Gallery, Boston, Massachusetts, 1977, 1979, 1982.
Tibor de Nagy Gallery, New York, 1957, 1958.
XXXII Biennale, Venice, Italy, 1964.
Ulrich Museum of Art, Wichita State University, Wichita, Kansas, 1980.
Waddington Galleries, Toronto, Canada, 1978, 1981.
Waddington Galleries II, London, England, 1970, 1973, 1979.
Watkins Gallery, American University, Washington, DC, 1950.
Watson/de Nagy & Co., Houston, Texas, 1975.

Bibliography

BOOKS

Alloway, Lawrence. *Network: Art and the Complex Present.* Ann Arbor, MI: University Microfilms, International Research Press, 1984.

American Artists on Art from 1940 to 1980. Edited by Ellen H. Johnson. New York: Harper & Row, Publishers, 1982, pp. 47-50.

Arnason, H.H. *History of Modern Art.* New York: Harry N. Abrams, Inc., 1968, pp. 620-625.

Ashton, Dore. *American Art Since 1945.* New York: Oxford University Press, 1982.

Ashton, Dore. *A Reading of Modern Art.* Cleveland, OH: Press of Case Western Reserve University, 1969, Part V, pp. 141-200.

Barnett, Vivian Endicott. *Handbook: The Guggenheim Museum Collection, 1900-1980.* New York: Solomon R. Guggenheim Foundation, 1980, pp. 496-97.

Battcock, Gregory. *Minimal Art – A Critical Anthology.* New York: E.P. Dutton & Co., Inc., 1968.

Burnham, J.W. "The Aesthetics of Intelligent Systems" in *On the Future of Art.* New York: Viking Press, 1970, pp. 98-99.

Calas, Nicolas and Elena. *Icons and Images of the Sixties.* New York: E.P. Dutton & Co., 1971, p. 187.

Chevreul, M(ichel) E(ugène). *The Principles of Harmony and Contrast of Colors.* London: Longman, Brown, Green, and Longman, 1885.

Duberman, Martin. *Black Mountain: An Exploration in Community.* New York: E.P. Dutton & Co., 1972, pp. 70-71, 244-245, 302, 428, 470.

Editors of Time-Life Books. *American Painting 1900-1970.* New York: Time Life Books, 1970, p. 183.

Fourcade, Dominique. *Helen Frankenthaler/Morris Louis/Kenneth Noland/Jules Olitski: Depuis la Couleur, 1958-1964.* Bordeaux, France: Centre d'Arts Plastiques Contemporains, 1981.

Geldzahler, Henry. *New York Painting and Sculpture: 1940-1970.* London: Pall Mall Press, Ltd., 1969, pp. 15, 21, 26, 27, 31-34, 37, 55, 370, 403-09, 411-17, 419, 422, 423, 425, 472.

Hunter, Sam. *La Pittura Americana del Dopoguerra.* Milan, Italy: Fratelli Fabbri Editori, 1970, pp. 14, 16.

Kozloff, Max. "Frank Stella and Kenneth Noland" in *Renderings: Critical Essays on a Century of Modern Art.* New York: Simon and Schuster, 1968, pp. 264-273.

Kramer, Hilton. *The Revenge of the Philistines; Art and Culture, 1972-1984.* New York: The Free Press, A Division of Macmillan, Inc., 1985, pp. 86, 200, 203-206, 225, 249.

Kultermann, Udo, *The New Painting.* New York: Frederick A. Praeger, Publishers, 1969.

Kuspit, Donald. *The Critic is Artist: The Intentionality of Art.* Ann Arbor, MI: University Microfilms International Research Press, 1984, p. 139.

Lucie-Smith, Edward. *Late Modern.* New York: Praeger, 1969, pp. 103, 107-110, 115.

Lukach, Joan M. *Hilla Rebay: In Search of the Spirit in Art.* New York: George Braziller, Inc., 1983, p. 169.

Moffett, Kenworth. *Kenneth Noland.* New York: Harry N. Abrams, Publisher, Inc., 1977.

Myers, John Bernard. *Tracking the Marvelous: A Life in the New York Art World.* New York: Random House, 1981, pp. 154, 199-201, 216.

Naylor, Colin, and Genesis P. Orridge, eds. *Contemporary Artists.* New York: St. Martin's Press, 1977.

Noland, Kenneth, in Paul Cummings, *Artists in Their Own Words.* New York: St. Martin's Press, 1979, p. 149.

Pincus-Witten, Robert. *Eye to Eye: Twenty Years of Art Criticism.* Ann Arbor, MI: University Microfilms International Research Press, 1984, pp. 39, 112, 119, 123, 226.

La Pintura de los Estados Unidos de Museos de la Ciudad de Washington. Mexico City, Mexico: Instituto Nacional de Bellas Artes, 1980, pp. 202-03.

Rood, Ogden N. *Modern Chromatics.* New York: D. Appleton and Co., 1881.

Rosenberg, Harold. *Art & Other Serious Matters.* Chicago: The University of Chicago Press, 1985, pp. 65, 117-124.

Russell, John. *The Meanings of Modern Art.* New York; Museum of Modern Art and Harper & Row, 1981, pp. 355-57.

Sandler, Irving. *The New York School: The Painters and Sculptors of the Fifties.* New York: Harper & Row, 1978.

Selz, Peter. *Art in our Times: A Pictorial History 1890-1980.* New York: Harry N. Abrams, 1981.

CATALOGS

Alley, Ronald. *Recent American Art.* London: Tate Gallery, 1969.

An American Choice. William S. Lieberman, ed. The Muriel Kallis Steinberg Newman Collection. Collection catalog. New York: Metropolitan Museum of Art, 1981.

Arkus, Leon Anthony. Introduction to *Pittsburgh International.* Exhibition catalog. Pittsburgh, PA: Museum of Art, Carnegie Institute, 1970, p. 66.

Arte Contemporaneo Norteamericano, Coleccion David Mirvish. Exhibition catalog. American Embassy in Madrid, 1984, p. 40.

Carmean, E.A., Jr. *The Great Decade, American Abstraction/Modernist Art 1960-1970.* Exhibition catalog. Houston, TX: Museum of Fine Art, 1974.

Color Abstractions: Selections from the Museum of Fine Arts. Introduction by Kenworth Moffett. Exhibition catalog. Boston, MA: Federal Reserve Bank of Boston, Display Area, 1979.

Colt, Priscilla. *Color and Field, 1890-1970.* Exhibition catalog. Buffalo, NY: Albright-Knox Art Gallery, Dayton Art Institute, Cleveland Museum, 1970, pp. 12 & 16.

Corcoran Gallery of Art. *The Catalogue of the Vincent Melzac Collection.* Exhibition catalog. Washington, DC: The Corcoran Gallery of Art, 1971.

Debrowski, Magdalena. *Contrasts of Form, Geometric Abstract Art, 1910-1980.* Exhibition catalog. New York: Museum of Modern Art, 1985.

Ellsworth Kelly, Morris Louis, Kenneth Noland, Frank Stella. Exhibition catalog. Chicago: The Museum of Contemporary Art, 1970.

Finch, Christopher. *Stella, Noland, Caro.* Exhibition catalog. Minneapolis, MN: Dayton's Gallery 12, 1969.

Fried, Michael. *Kenneth Noland.* Exhibition catalog. New York: The Jewish Museum, 1965.

Fried, Michael. *Three American Painters: Kenneth Noland, Jules Olitski, Frank Stella.* Exhibition catalog. Cambridge, MA: Fogg Art Museum, 1965.

Geldzahler, Henry. *Kenneth Noland: Winds, Painted Monotypes.* New York: André Emmerich Gallery, 1983.

Geldzahler, Henry. *New York Painting and Sculpture: 1940-1970.* Exhibition catalog. New York: Metropolitan Museum of Art, 1970.

Goossen, E.C. *Kenneth Noland.* Exhibition catalog. Bennington, VT: Bennington College, 1961.

Goossen, E.C. *Kenneth Noland.* Exhibition catalog. Zurich, Switzerland: Galerie Charles Lienhard, 1962.

Greenberg, Clement. *Kenneth Noland.* Exhibition catalog. London: Kasmin Ltd., 1963.

Helen Frankenthaler, Paintings on Paper. Exhibition catalog. San Francisco, CA: John Berggruen Gallery, 1986.

Hudson, Andrew. *Ten Washington Artists: 1950-1970.* Exhibition catalog. Edmonton, Canada: Edmonton Art Gallery, 1970, pp. 6-7, 10-11, 16-17.

Hunter, Sam. *Masters of the Fifties: American Abstract Painting from Pollock to Stella.* Exhibition catalog. New York: Marisa del Re Gallery, 1985.

Janis, Eugenia, P. *Paper Forms: Hand-Made Paper Projects.* Catalog review. Cambridge, MA: Massachusetts Institute of Technology, Hayden Gallery, 1977.

Kenneth Noland. Exhibition catalog. New York: André Emmerich Gallery, 1962.

Kenneth Noland. Exhibition catalog. New York: André Emmerich Gallery, 1971.

Kenneth Noland. Exhibition catalog. New York: French & Co., 1959.

Kenneth Noland. Exhibition catalog. Paris, France: Galerie Lawrence, 1963.

Kenneth Noland. Exhibition catalog. Zurich, Switzerland: Galerie Renée Ziegler, 1969.

Kenneth Noland in Paris, 1984. Essay by Ann Hindry. Exhibition catalog. Paris: Galerie de France, 1984.

Kenneth Noland, New Paintings. Exhibition catalog. New York: André Emmerich Gallery, Inc., 1973.

Kenneth Noland: New Paintings. Exhibition catalog. New York: André Emmerich Gallery, 1983.

Kenneth Noland, New Paintings. Exhibition catalog. New York: André Emmerich Gallery, 1984.

Kenneth Noland: Recent Paperworks. Essay by Elizabeth Higdon. Exhibition catalog. Durham, NC: Duke University Museum of Art, 1983.

Kenneth Noland "Vientos" (Winds). Essay by Henry Galdzahler. Exhibition catalog. Mexico City, Mexico: Museo de Arte Moderno, Taller de Grafica Mexicana, S.A., 1983.

Kenneth Noland: Winds, Painted Monotypes. Essay by Henry Geldzahler. Exhibition catalog. New York: André Emmerich Gallery, 1983.

Kozloff, Max. *Twenty-Five Years of American Painting, 1948-1973.* Exhibition catalog. Des Moines, IA: Des Moines Art Center, 1973.

Kuspit, Donald B. *Out of the South: An Exhibition of Work by Artists Born in the South.* Exhibition catalog. Atlanta, GA: Heath Gallery, 1982, pp. 18-19.

Lussier, Real. *Artistes Américains Contemporains.* Exhibition catalog. Montreal, Canada: Musée d'Art Contemporain, 1978.

McCabe, Cynthia Jaffe. *Artistic Collaboration in the Twentieth Century.* Exhibition catalog. Washington DC: Hirshhorn Museum and Sculpture Garden, 1984, pp. 169-170.

New York New Art Now 85, ARCA Marseille. Introduction by Roger Pailhas. Exhibition catalog. Marseille, France, ARCA Centre d'Art Contemporain, 1985.

Noland, Kenneth. "Kenneth Noland at Emma Lake, 1963" in *Ten Washington Artists: 1950-1970, Morris Louis, Kenneth Noland, Gene Davis, Thomas Downing,*

Howard Mehring, Sam Gilliam, Blaine Larson, Michael Clark, J.L. Knight, Rockne Krebs. Exhibition catalog. Edmonton, Alberta, Canada: Edmonton Art Gallery, 1970.

Pre Postmodern, Good in the Art of Our Time. Exhibition catalog. Richard F. Brush Art Gallery, St. Lawrence University, 1985.

Selections from the William J. Hokin Collection. Exhibition catalog. Chicago: Museum of Contemporary Art, 1985.

Shulman, Leon. *The Direct Image.* Exhibition catalog. Worcester, MA: Worcester Art Museum, 1969.

Sundell, Nina. *The Robert and Jane Meyerhoff Collection.* Collection catalog. Privately published, 1980; pp. 42-43.

Twentieth Century Works of Art. Exhibition catalog. New York: Stephen Mazoh & Co., Inc., 1985.

Upright, Diane. *Grand Compositions: Selections from the Collection of David Mirvish.* Exhibition catalog. Fort Worth, TX: The Fort Worth Art Museum, 1985.

Upright, Diane. *Morris Louis: The Complete Paintings.* Catalog raisonné. New York: Harry N. Abrams, Inc., Publishers, 1985.

Waldman, Diane. *Kenneth Noland: A Retrospective.* Exhibition catalog. New York: Solomon R. Guggenheim Museum, 1977.

Wilkin, Karen. Introduction to *Kenneth Noland.* Exhibition catalog. Edmonton, Alberta, Canada: Edmonton Art Gallery, 1975.

With Paper, About Paper. Exhibition catalog. Buffalo, NY: Albright-Knox Art Gallery, 1980, pp. 11, 56-57.

INTERVIEWS

Noland, Kenneth. Interview with Richard H. Love, 29 October, 1985. Videorecording. American Art Forum with Richard Love, Chicago.

Noland, Kenneth. Interview with Richard H. Love, April 1986. R.H. Love Galleries Archives, Chicago.

PERIODICALS

"After Abstract Expressionism." *Art International,* 6, no. 8 (October 1962), pp. 24-29.

Allen, Jane Addams. "Time Tests the Artists' Insights." *The Washington Times,* 12 November 1982.

Alloway, Lawrence. "Easel Painting at the Guggenheim." *Art International,* 5, no. 10 (December 1961), pp. 26-34.

Ameringer, Will. "Kenneth Noland." *Arts Magazine,* 56 (May 1982), p. 3.

"Art — Noland: The Spectrum is the Message." *Time,* 18 April 1969, pp. 74-75.

Ashbery, John. "Paris Notes." *Art International,* 5, nos. 5-6 (June-August 1961), pp. 42, 92.

Ashton, Dore. "Esempi Recenti di Pittura non Oggettiva Negli Stati Uniti." *L'Arte Moderna,* 13, no. 111, pp. 81-120.

Ashton, Dore. "Exhibition at the Emmerich Gallery." *International Studio,* 171 (May 1966), p. 206.

Ashton, Dore. "Visual Pleasure from Austerity." *Studio International,* 169, no. 862 (February 1965), pp. 92-93.

Bannard, Walter. "Noland's New Paintings." *Artforum,* 10 (November 1971), pp. 50-53.

Bannard, Walter. "Notes on American Painting of the Sixties." *Artforum,* 8 (January 1970), pp. 40-45.

Baro, Gene. "London Letter." *Art International,* 9, no. 5 (June 1965), pp. 67-70.

Benson, Legrace G. "The Washington Scene." *Art International,* 13, no. 10 (Christmas 1969), pp 21-23, 36-42, 50.

Bourdon, David. "Rückzug aus dem Olymp: Kenneth Noland Retrospektive in Guggenheim Museum, New York." *Du,* August 1977, p. 14.

Breerette, Genevieve. "Quatre abstraits américains à Bordeaux." *Le Monde,* 12 March 1981, p. 15.

Brooks, Valerie F., and Nilson Lisbet. "The Art Market: A Question of Quality." *Artnews,* 81, no. 2 (February 1982), pp. 8, 11.

Calas, Nicolas. "Maximal & Minimal Constructivism and Structures." *Arts Magazine,* 42 (June/Summer 1968), 42.

"Canvases Brimming with Color". *Life Magazine,* 24 (September 1971), p. 74.

Carmean, E.A. Jr. "Celebrating the Birth of Stain Painting." *The Washington Post,* 26 October 1982, p. B7.

Carpenter, Ken. "To Re-Examine The Work of Kenneth Noland". *Studio International,* 188, no. 968 (July-August 1974), pp. 21-26.

Cavaliere, Barbara. "Kenneth Noland". *Arts Magazine,* 53, no. 5 (January 1979), p. 20.

"Ces douze peintres ont un point commun." *Connaissance des Arts,* no. 229 (March 1971), p. 133.

Clurman, Irene. "Artist Kenneth Noland Offers No Easy Answers." *Rocky Mountain News,* 2 April 1978, p. 16.

"A Company Graph with a Difference." *Corporate Artnews,* May-June 1985, pp. 9, 10.

Cone, Jane Harrison. "Kenneth Noland's New Paintings." *Artforum,* 6, no. 3 (November 1967), pp 36-41.

Cone, Jane Harrison. "On Color in Kenneth Noland's Paintings." *Art International,* 9, no. 5 (June 1965), pp. 36-38.

Coplans, John. "Serial Imagery." *Artforum,* 7, no. 2 (October 1968), pp. 34-43.

Coulonges, Henri. "Beauté suave." *Connaissance des Arts,* no. 229 (March 1971), p. 81.

Deschamps, Madeleine. "Depuis la couleur." *Art Press 44,* January 1981, pp. 24-25.

Denver, Bernard. "Hans Hofmann & Kenneth Noland at the Waddington Gallery". *Studio International,* September 1973, p. 107, 108.

Deschamps, Madeleine. "Surfaces et supports des années 60: la post-painterly abstraction." *Art Press 36,* April 1980, pp. 26-27.

Elderfield, John. "Abstract Painting in the Seventies". *Art International,* 16, nos. 6-7, (Summer 1972), p. 92.

Elderfield, John. "Mondrian, Newman, Noland: Two Notes on Changing Style." *Artforum,* 10, no. 4 (December 1971), pp. 48-53.

"Exhibition at Rubin Gallery." *Artnews,* 68 (Summer 1969), p. 20.

"Exhibition at Tibor de Nagy Gallery." *Arts Magazine,* 31 (February 1957), p. 65.

"First One-Man Show of Oils in New York at De Nagy Gallery." *Art News,* 55 (February 1957), p. 10.

Forgey, Benjamin. "In the Wake of the Washington Color School." *Washington Star,* 2 October 1977, p. 1.

Forgey, Benjamin. "Now There's a Painting Gap." *The Evening Star* (Washington, DC), 18 December 1970, C.10.

Freed, Eleanor. "A Windfall for Texas." *Art in America,* 57, no. 6 (November-December 1969), pp. 78-85.

Fried, Michael. "Anthony Caro and Kenneth Noland: Some Notes on Not Composing." *The Lugano Review,* I, no. 3-4 (Summer 1965), pp. 198-206.

Fried, Michael. "New York Letter." *Art International, 6,* no. 8 (October 1962), p. 70.

Fried, Michael. "New York Letter." *Art International, 7,* no. 5 (May 1963), pp. 69-71.

Fried, Michael. "Recent Work by Kenneth Noland." *Artforum, 7* (Summer 1969), pp. 36-37.

"Galerie Renée Ziegler, Zürich." *Werk, Bauen & Wohnen,* 57 (March 1970), p. 207.

Glaberson, Barbara. "Kenneth Noland." *Art World,* November 1983, p. 6.

Glueck, Grace. "The 20th Century Artists Most Admired by Other Artists." *Artnews,* 76, no. 9 (November 1977), p. 78.

Goldstein, Carl. "Teaching Modernism: What Albers Learned in the Bauhaus and Taught to Rauschenberg, Noland, and Hesse." *Arts Magazine* 54, no. 4 (December 1979), pp. 108-116.

Gordon, A. "Art in the Modern Manner." *Connoisseur,* 169 (September 1968), p. 38.

Gouk, Alan. "An Essay on Painting." *Studio International,* October 1970, p. 146.

Greenberg, Clement. "After Abstract Expressionism." *Art International,* 6, no. 8 (October 1962), p. 24.

Greenberg, Clement. "Louis and Noland." *Art International,* 4, no. 5 (May 1960), pp. 26-29.

Greenberg, Clement. "Poetry of Vision." *Artforum,* April 1968, pp. 20-22.

Harrison, Jane. "On Color in Kenneth Noland's Painting." *Art International,* 9, no. 5 (June 1965), pp. 36-38.

Henning, Edward B. "Color and Field." *Art International,* 15 (20 May 1971), pp. 46-50.

Henry, Gerritt. "Kenneth Noland at André Emmerich." *Art in America,* 71, no. 6 (Summer 1983), pp. 157-158.

Henry, Gerritt. "Paper in Transition." *The Print Collector's Newsletter,* X, no. 3 (July-August 1979), p. 84.

Hess, Thomas B. "Kenneth Noland, Hesitant Prophet." *New York Magazine,* 23 May 1977, pp. 76-78.

Hess, Thomas B. "Phony Crisis in American Art." *Art News,* 62 (Summer 1963), p. 60.

"Hitting the Bullseye." *Newsweek,* LIX, no. 16 (16 April 1962), p. 108.

Hudson, Andrew. "Letter From Washington." *Art International* 9, nos. 9-10 (December 1965), p. 56.

Hudson, Andrew. "The 1967 Pittsburgh International." *Art International,* 11, no. 1 (Christmas 1967), pp. 57-64.

Hughes, Robert. "Pure Uncluttered Hedonism." *Time Magazine,* 2 May 1977.

"In the Museums, Kenneth Noland, Morris Louis and Anthony Caro." *Arts Magazine,* 42 (June-Summer 1968).

"Jackson Pollock: An Artists' Symposium." *Artnews,* 66, no. 3 (May 1967), p. 27.

Jacobs, J. "Collector: Joseph H. Hirshhorn." *Art in America,* 57 (July 1969), p. 65.

Jenkins, Mark. "Kenneth Noland's Endlessly Charming Paintings." *Unicorn Times,* November 1977, p. 59.

Judd, Don. "New York Letter." *Art International* 9, no. 3 (April 1965), p. 37.

Kaufman, Betty. "Noland's Pitch." *Art World,* 2, no. 4, (December 1977-January 1978).

"Kenneth Noland's Market." *The Artnewsletter,* 3 May 1983, pp. 5, 6.

Kerber, B. "Streifenbilder; zur Unterscheidung ähnlicher Phänomene." *Wallraf - Richartz - Jahrbuch,* 32 (1970), pp. 235-256.

Kingsley, April. "Galleries: Out-of-the-Ordinary Mixed Bags." *The Village Voice,* 2 January 1978, p. 66.

Kosloff, Max. *The Nation,* 18 December 1967, pp. 667-669.

Kramer, Hilton. "Art: Landmarks on the Color Field." *The New York Times,* 22 April 1977.

Kramer, Hilton. "The Metropolitan Takes Another Step Forward." *The New York Times,* 25 May 1968, p. 31.

Kramer, Hilton. "Modernist Show Moves Met Firmly into Art of 20th Century." *The New York Times,* 22 May 1981.

Kramer, Hilton. "Review." *The New York Times,* 18 November 1967.

Krauss, Rosalind E. "On Frontality." *Artforum,* 6, no. 9 (May 1968), pp. 40-46.

Leider, Phillip. "Gallery '68." *Look Magazine,* 32, no. 1 (9 January 1968), pp. 14, 18.

Leider, Phillip. "New York — The Art of the Real." *Artforum,* 7, no. 1 (September 1968), p. 65.

Lewis, Jo Ann. "Noland's Paper Art." *Washington Post,* 30 October 1982.

Lewis, Jo Ann. "The SoHo Connection." *The Washington Post,* 29 November 1981, p. G1, G11.

Lord, B. "Three American Painters Tour Canada." *Canadian Art* 23 (July 1968), p. 50.

McCaughey, Patrick. "Pictorialism and Some Recent Sculpture." *Arts Magazine,* Summer 1971, pp. 21-22.

McConoghau, Al. "Noland Wants His Painting to Exist as Sensation." *Minneapolis Tribune,* 13 March 1966, p. 4.

Mackie, Alwynne. "Kenneth Noland and Quality in Art." *Art International,* Summer 1979, pp. 40-45, 52-53.

Masheck, Joseph. "Sorting Out the Whitney Annual." *Artforum* 9 (February 1971), p. 72.

Melville, R. "Minimalism." *Architectural Review,* 146 (August 1969), p. 146.

Moffett, Kenworth. "Kenneth Noland's New Paintings and the Issue of the Shaped Canvas." *Art International,* 20, nos. 4-5 (April-May 1976).

Moffett, Kenworth. "Noland Vertical." *Artnews,* 70, no. 6 (October 1971), pp. 48-49, 76-78.

Newman, Patricia. "New Processes Add Tangible Shape to Venerable Art Form." *The Smithsonian,* August 1980, pp. 60-64.

"New York Commentary: Conditioned Historic Reactions." *Studio International,* 171, no. 877 (May 1966), p. 206.

Nodelman, Sheldon. "Sixties Art: Some Philosophical Perspectives." *The Yale Architectural Journal-Perspecta II,* pp. 73-89.

"Noland's New Paintings." *Artforum,* 10, no. 3 (November 1971), pp. 50-53.

North, Percy. "Generations of the Washington Color School." *Washington Review,* 10, no. 3 (October-November 1984), p. 24.

Overy, Paul. "Reviews." *The London Times,* 5 December 1975.

Page, Tim. "Contemporary Painters Devise a Concert Program." *The New York Times,* 10 November 1985, pp. C21, C26.

"Painting by Kenneth Noland." *St. Louis Museum Bulletin* 2 (November 1966), p. 6.

Patton, Phil. "A Master of Abstract Painting — Kenneth Noland." *Eastern Review,* June 1979, pp. 74-79.

Peppiatt, Michael. "Sujet Tabou: Exposition Risquée." *Connaissance des Arts,* September 1984.

Polcari, Stephen. "Kenneth Noland: Independence in the Face of Conformity." *Artnews* 76, no. 6 (Summer 1977), pp. 153-155.

Pomeroy, Ralph. "New York." *Art and Artists,* 2, no. 10 (January 1968), p. 43.

Prak, Niels Luning. "Persistent Schemes: The Quest for a Neutral Form." *Art International* 14 (September 1970), pp. 76-78.

Rand, Harry. "Recent Painting: A Rambling Contemplation." *Arts Magazine* 56, no. 8 (April 1982), pp. 106-109.

Ratcliff, Carter. "New York Letter." *Art International,* 15, no. 10, (20 December 1971), p. 59.

Rees, R.J. "Kenneth Noland." *Studio International,* January-February 1975.

Reise, Barbara M. "Greenberg and the Group: A Retrospective View." *Studio International,* Part 1, 175, no. 900, (May 1968), pp. 254-257; Part 2, 175, no. 901 (June 1968), p. 314-315.

Richard, Paul. "But Not Forgotten." *Washington Post,* 26 December 1970, pp. B1, B3.

Richard, Paul. "Full Circle for Noland." *The Washington Post,* 4 May 1982, pp. C1-2.

Richard, Paul. "Look Who's Back, Letting Color Sing." *The Washington Post,* 30 September 1977.

Richard, Paul. "Portrait: Washington, DC." *Portfolio,* June-July 1979, pp. 82-87.

Richard, Paul. "$300,000 Surprise: Kenneth Noland's Washington Color Canvas Hits the Bull's-Eye." *Washington Post,* 21 November 1981, p. C1.

Ronnen, Meir. "Kenneth Noland." *The Jerusalem Post Magazine,* November 1977, p. 20.

Rose, Barbara. "Kenneth Noland." *Art International,* 8 nos. 5-6 (Summer 1964), pp. 58-63.

Rose, Barbara. "Vogue's Spotlight Art — New York Season, 'A Breather' ". *Vogue Magazine,* 151, no. 10 (June 1968), p. 78.

Rubin, William. "Younger American Painters." *Art International,* 4, no. 1 (January 1960), pp. 28-29.

Russell, John. "Art: In Show of New Noland Paintings, Consistency Takes Unexpected Forms." *The New York Times,* 22 November 1975.

Russell, John. "Review." *The New York Times,* 7 November 1980, p. C20.

Russell, John. "Review. Emmerich." *The New York Times,* 5 June 1981.

Russell, John. "A Show to Lighten Your Step and Bring Smiles." *The New York Times,* June 1977, pp. 29, 34.

Schjeldahl, P. "New York Letter." *Art International* 13, no. 6 (Summer 1969), pp. 64-65.

Stevens, E. "Washington Color Painters." *Arts Magazine* 40 (November 1965), p. 30.

Stevens, Mark. "Noland's Garden of Color." *Newsweek,* 16 May 1977, p. 72.

Tallmer, Jerry. "Diamonds of the '50s Bring It All Back." *New York Post,* 16 April 1977, p. 22.

Tatransky, Valentin. "Group Show, Knoedler." *Arts Magazine,* 54, no. 6 (February 1980), pp. 36-37.

Tatransky, Valentin. "Kenneth Noland: As Great as Ever." *Arts Magazine,* 57, no. 10 (June 1983), pp. 118-119.

Tillim, Sidney. "Evaluations and Re-Evaluations, A Season's End Miscellany . . . ." *Artforum,* 6, no. 10 (Summer 1968), pp. 20-23.

Tillim, Sidney. "Scale and the Future of Modernism." *Artforum,* 7, no. 2 (October 1968), pp. 14-18.

Truitt, James McC. "Art-Arid D.C. Harbors Touted 'New Painters' ". *The Washington Post,* 21 December 1961, p. A20.

Tuchman, Phyllis. "American Art in Germany; The History of a Phenomenon." *Artforum* 9 (November 1970), p. 67.

Tuchman, Phyllis. "Architectural Digest Visits Kenneth Noland." *Architectural Digest,* July 1985, pp. 110-115.

Waldman, Diane. "Color, Format and Abstract Art: An Interview with Kenneth Noland." *Art in America,* 65, no. 3 (May-June 1977), pp. 99-105.

Whitford, Frank, and Robert Kudielka. "Documenta 4, A Critical Review." *Studio International,* September 1968, pp. 74-78.

Weinstein, David. "Noland and Zox at Emmerich." *Art in America,* 61, no. 5 (September-October 1973), pp. 94-96.

Wright, Martha McWilliams. "Washington." *Art International,* 22, no. 1 (January 1978), pp. 61-67.

Wykes-Joyce, Max. "Art in London: Six New Exhibitions." *International Herald Tribune,* 20-21 June 1970, p. 7.

Widely known for his expertise as an art historian, art dealer, lecturer, and television personality, Richard H. Love effectively combines scholarship, experience, and original interpretation in his writings. With his background as former professor of art history and as a successful art dealer who is in touch with countless sources on art history throughout the United States and overseas, the author has written several fascinating books on American artists. He explored a pioneering American impressionist in *Mary Cassatt: The Independent* and presented a great talent from the recent past in *Harriet Randall Lumis: 1870-1953, An American Impressionist.* With *John Barber: The Artist, the man,* the author delivered an intriguing story of a unique twentieth-century American painter of social realism.

In spite of his hectic business schedule and numerous civic involvements, Richard Love manages to produce a veritable flood of essays on exhibiting artists. A recently completed study has resulted in *The Sculpture of John Cunningham: Image – Space – Interval,* an exhibition catalog with a valuable analysis of the artist's work. In *Tom Torluemke: Images from Ultrasound,* the author presents incisive views of a talented and innovative young artist from Chicago. Richard Love's latest major publication, *Theodore Earl Butler: Emergence from Monet's Shadow,* is an exhaustive story of America's foremost pioneering post-impressionist and the art world of his time.

Out of his devotion to American art, Richard Love has launched a unique television talk show, the "American Art Forum with Richard Love," which features artists, art critics, art movements, and in general enlightens the public about American artistic creativity.

Photography: Steven Sloman, Wayne McCall, T.K. Rose
Research and Editorial Preparation: Vytautas Babusis
Design: Bruce C. Bachman
Printing: The Argus Press Inc.
Typesetting and Layout: Graphic House Enterprises